Aphorisms & Poems of Light

Jacob Oketch

Dani Tegan Inc.

ISBN: 978-1-7352657-0-4

DEDICATION

This collection is dedicated, first and foremost to my beloved big sister Dr. Hellen Oketch-Rabah who has, over the years, been a great source of encouragement to me, in my nascent writing career. Even when I have been on the verge of giving up, she always reignited my creative spirit. She is the only member of my family who unreservedly believe in my creative abilities and has made the publication of this work possible.
I am also indebted to my boss, Mrs Muthoni Likimani, one of Kenya's oldest writers. At 94 years of age, she continues to pen titles to the awe of the younger generation of writers. Her zeal and commitment greatly inspire me in my creative journey.
Lastly, this work is inspired by the many writers I have interacted with. The many workshops and seminars I have taken part in, has given me an opportunity to brush shoulders with many accomplished writers who have kept the creative fire burning in me. Their mentorship has been most valuable.

CONTENTS

ACKNOWLEDGMENTS

First, I would like to express my gratitude to Noni's Publicity, for enabling me to process my manuscript. I am also indebted to Mr. Benson Shiholo for his editorial advice on how to improve the manuscript.

I sincerely thank my sister Dr. Hellen Oketch-Rabar for going through the manuscript and making the necessary adjustments. My brother Johnstone Summit and my other sister Beatrice Oketch have also been incredibly supportive both morally and materially. My nephew Bill Oketch has been particularly good to me in my darkest moments in life and I immensely thank him for believing in me.I also shared the raw manuscript with my fellow poet Ngwatilo Mawiyoo and I thank her for going through my raw work before publication.

This work would not have seen the light of day without the constant encouragement from my former classmate in college, the late Prof Ken Walibora, a renowned author who tragically passed on early this year. His demise greatly fueled my determination to follow in his footsteps as an honour to him

Lastly, I am grateful to the PEN-Kenya fraternity where I am serving as the treasurer, for their continued encouragement. I would like to single out the President, Khainga Okwemba, Secretary General, Tony Mochama and the late Prof Chris Lukorito Wanjala, for steadfastly walking with me on the journey towards the publication of this work. The many trips we undertook in high schools across the country, together with creative writers, to promote literature, entrenched in me, the determination to publish my work.

1 SOMEONE WALKED THROUGH A WALL

Someone walked through a wall
You don’t believe me
Then wait for me
At street 69 mapambano
To see for yourself

How can you believe
That Jesus Christ flew to heaven
By looking at his footprints
And yet refuse
To believe
That someone walked through a wall
Believe me
Someone walked through a wall.

The impregnable wall
Can be brought down
Do you remember the one
That was erected in Berlin?
Where is it?
Why walls and wails
Of separation?
Someone walked through a wall
Banish the walls

That separate our dreams
From cementing
Into one big mould
Of success
Someone walked through a wall
Did you see him
I did.

∞

2. DONT BE AFRAID

Don’t be afraid
Of what looks like you
Because it is you
Only dressed in another attire

Don’t be afraid of yourself
By fearing somebody else
We are all the same
No one
Bears the soul of God
But of man

Unshackle yourself
From the chain of illusion
That tears your courage
From seeing the truth
As it is
Truth is naked
Be honest

∞

3. THE CONFRONTATION

When you are confronted
By a vile energy
Smile
And breath in
When you beath out
You feel
What it means
To climb down
From the gates of hell
Into an open field
Of heavenly bliss.

4. I WILL NOT BEG

I will not beg
When my wealth
Is safely and firmly tucked
In my soul.

∞

5. SOMETIMES

Sometimes
The truth changes
It just depends
Upon where you are standing
Is it a fresh place?

6. IMAGINE MORE

You can never be stuck
Because the universe
Is ever expanding

All you need to do
Is look less
And imagine more

Do you want your life
To manifest
As you see it
Or as you imagine it?

∞

7. FEEL GOOD

Feeling good
Is the only way
To align yourself
To the source energy

The only reason
For yearning for
ANYTHING
Is to feel good

So endeavour
To feel good
AT ALL TIMES
For it is the gateway
To all that you desire.

∞

8. IT IS UPTO YOU

What happened yesterday
Does not matter today
Unless
You are still thinking about it

In this fresh place
Where I stand
NOW
Is what matters
And the universe expands

Do you want to recreate the past?
Or do you want
To feel good now
And create a perfect future?
It is all upto you

∞

9. WELLBEING

The only force that exists
Is that of wellbeing
It flows
Whether you Aare aware of it
Or not

You came to this universe
By choice
And you can never be disconnected
completely
From the source energy

But because
You have picked up
Resistance tendencies
To your wellbeing
You continue searching for it
When it is always hovering around you.

∞

10. REMEMBER

Once you remember
That you are love,freedom
And joy

Once you remember
That you are creative,powerful
And that all is well

Your journey
To the fulfillment
Of your desires
Will be much shorter
Than you expected.

∞

11. UNTITLED

When you appreciate
You allow
When you criticize
You resist

When you meditate
You raise your point
Of vibration
By expelling
Undesired thoughts

Don't you know
Why we sing chants and praises
Give thanks.

∞

12. YOUR WISH IS MY COMMAND

What you intend
You focus on
And create

Don't think about it
If you don't want to create it

Don't look at it
If you don't want to create it

Don't speak about it
If you don't want to create it

Don't remember it
If you don't want to create it

Don't imagine it
If you don't want to create it

Within you
Is the force

That creates reality
So

Be careful
About what you wish for.

13. UNTITLED

You didn't come into this world
To change it
But to be a part
Of this magical, creative experience
For everything that exists
Is there for a purpose
Unique
To themselves

If you are purpose-driven
Find it
In yourself
For that indeed
Is where it is.

∞

14. PENFORCE

When you write something
Imagining
That it is happening
You call forth
A powerful creative force
That makes it
BECOME

The power of the pen
Springs forth
From the creative force
That governs
ALL
That the universe
Is all about
Pen
Your reality.

∞

15. IT IS POSSIBLE

It is possible
To delegate
What you cannot do
To the universe
And it will be done

Yes
You don't need to do everything
To create reality
If only you knew.

∞

16. AVERT THE CALAMITY

Have you woken up
And recalled a bad dream?
Then you must do something about it.
Because if you don't
Then what you experienced
In the dream
Will happen in future
Secure your future
By changing the bad experience
In your dream
To a good one
By changing
The direction
Of your thoughts.

∞

17. I AM FREE

I am free
To allow
The most joyous feeling
Into my experience

I am free
To create my own reality

I am free
To ask the source energy
To fulfill all my desires
I am free
To call forth
Abundance
In my life

I am free
To be
Do
Or have
Anything I want.

∞

18. ETERNAL BEING

Before I was born
I was there
After I die
I will be there
I am eternal

Recoiling back
To where I really belong
I unsheathe myself
Of the baggage of this world
And return I
To the truest and freshest place
Eternity

I am
Beyond
What I appear to be.

∞

19. NO MATTER....

No matter what you are going through
Wellbeing flows

No matter where you are
Wellbeing flows

No matter how you feel
Wellbeing flows

No matter what people think about you
Wellbeing flows

No matter what happens
In the entire universe
Wellbeing flows

Wellbeing flows
Because
It is the only thing
That there is
EVER.

∞

20. THE GATEWAY

You do not lack
What you desire
Because it has not been offered
To you

You lack
What you desire
Because
You are yet
To allow it
Into your experience

Listen
To your inner voice
It will guide you
To the road
To fulfillment.

∞

21. I CREATE

I imagine
I am with her

I think
I am with her

I remember
I was with her

I know
I am with her

I am with her
Here.

∞

22. THE SELF

It is not so much about
The size of your home
For that is a given
That results
From the accumulation
Of one's desires

Nor isnt it
About respect
From others

It
Is about
The respect
Of the self
The true repository
Of spiritual abundance
The mother
Of all abundance
On planet earth.

∞

23. NO ONE BUT YOU

No one
But you
Knows what is best
For you
Because no one
But you
Feels the vibrational content
Of your desires

No one but you
Holds the key
To unlocking
The floodgate
Of the manifestation
Of your desires

No one
But you
Can know
Who you really are.

∞

24. THE MIRROR

The main purpose
For your existence
In this universe
Is to truly realize
Who you truly are

How do you expect
To fulfill this mission
When
Most of the time
Your attention
Is riveted
On other things
Other than yourself

It is not possible
To see your image
While you are looking
Elsewhere
Other than the mirror.

∞

25. I AM ENSLAVED TO GRANT YOUR WISH

Did you know
That I became
Your slave
When you decided
To come into this universe

Did you know
That I will not stop
Being your slave
Even when you say no
Because serving you
Is all I ever wanted.

∞

26. FORM AND CONTENT

The roof
Holds the house

The ground
Holds the grass

The song
Holds the story

The body
Holds the soul

The mother
Holds the child
The seed
Holds the forest

The poem
Holds the truth

In form
Is the content.

∞

27. ONCE YOU SURRENDER

Once you surrender
You have allowed
Your inner being
To reveal itself
To you

Once you surrender
You open the vista
And discover
The magical possibilities
That inhabit
Your psyche

Once you surrender
You realize
That you are not here
To change the world
But yourself

Once you surrender
You finally discover
The power of allowing
Because it will net you
All your desires
And make you

Be, do or have
Whatever you desire
It is time to surrender.

28. NO END

I know
That my soul
Will not end
Even when I disappear
From this world
Because
It will be waiting for me
On the other side.

29. DO NOT FIX IT

You cannot fix
What you did not make
So
Stop trying
To change the world
For God

Is all that you see
Both wanted
And unwanted
Peer into self
And see redemption.

30. THERE IS ENOUGH

There cannot be competition
Where resources
Are enough for everybody
So
Why squabble
Over what we already have
In abundance

There is no lack
There is no shortage
Because the universe expands
Everytime you ask
The pie is enough.

∞

31. ANGER RELIEVES

To be angry
In order to relieve yourself
Of depression
Is the first step
To regaining your connection
To the source energy

So
Vent it out
And move up
To where you naturally belong
Wellness
And wellbeing.

∞

32. POWER

Real power
Is vested in you
And not
In institutions
Harness it
And be
Your own leader
For you don't need a title
To be a leader.

∞

33. SELF CREATION

It is not
What other people think
About yourself
That matters
But
What you think
About yourself.

Create
Your own reality
The way you want it
By believing
In the power
Of your own thoughts.

∞

34. JUMP TO RELIEF

Whenever a troubling thought
Invades you
Jump to another one
It will never come back
Unless
You allow it to
And if it comes back
Jump to another thought
Keep on jumping
Untill you reach
A better feeling place
That is the journey
To your bliss.

∞

35. I APPRECIATE

I appreciate
My eternal connection
To the source energy

I will continue appreciating
The beauties of this world
In order to maintain
My connection
To the source energy.

36. ALWAYS

Source energy
ALWAYS
Intends wellbeing
Anything else
Is your own creation.

∞

37. WORST ENEMY

Nobody can stop
You
From achieving
What you were destined
To achieve
By source energy

It is only you
Who CAN.

∞

38. IMAGINE AND MAKE

Do you want
To see the world
The way it is

Or,
Do you want
To see the world
The way you imagine it

Imagine
A different world
From what you are seeing
For it is the onset
Of deliberate creation
I choose it.

∞

39. EXCLUSIVE CONTRACT

It does not matter
Whether I was born
In a palace
Or a manger

What matters
Is that I was born

That birth
Confirmed my desire
To be in this world

No one
But me
Knows who I am
For this was a contract
Between me
And God
EXCLUSIVELY
Sorry
There is no intercession.

∞

40. PRIORITY

Never do anything
For anyone
Other than yourself
Because
They can do everything
For themselves.

41. ENJOY AT ALL TIMES

How can I do
Something
That I do not enjoy
For that amounts
To robbing myself
Of the essence of living

Joy
Is at the top
Of my priority list
In this life
All the time

I cannot do
Without joy
Because
It is the gateway
To abundance.

42. EGOTRAP

Ego
Is a stumbling block
Between you
And the real enjoyment
Of life

When you get
Past your ego
You recognize
That whatever you are doing
Is just a role

The real you
Is unknown by anybody
But you.

∞

43. IT ONLY TAKES A SECOND

It only takes a second
To vibrate differently
And feel good
Just try it
Because feeling good
Is the ultimate
And truest purpose
Of life.

44. LOVE STILLS

A feeling
Of love
Is as mysterious
As life itself
So
It demands
A certain subservience
To the beckoning forces
Who are only asking
For non resistance
And then
Voila...

It happens.
A perfect vibrational match
What an amazing stuff.

45. DELICATE SOUL

There comes a time
When the soul
Becomes malleable

That is when
Light appears
At the end of the tunnel

Traversing the unknown
The soul expands
In amazing ways
Supplicating
To the will
Of wellbeing.

∞

46. THERE IS NOTHING TO ANYTHING

Life
Is not worth fighting for
But living

When you find yourself
Struggling to live
Still yourself
To a state of surrender
And relief emerges
For non resistance
ALWAYS
Yields
The manifestation
Of your desires

There is nothing
To anything
For wellbeing
Guarantees
Wellness
For ALL.

Nothing
Is more important

Than vibrating appropriately
Breath properly.

47. NOW IS WHAT MATTERS

Never plan
For tomorrow
For NOW
Is waiting for you

Over here
Is more real
Than over there

48. ENERGY DOES NOT DECEIVE

Perfect coincidences
Are a manifestation
Of a vibrational match
That defines
Magical experiences.
It is time
To get used to them
For energy
Cannot deceive.

49. LOOKS LIE

My looks
Do not constitute
My soul

So
What I breath and speak
Precedes
My physical appearance

My wellbeing
Will not be dictated
By my attire
But the purity
Of my thoughts

I strive
To think beauty
And perfection
Even when I am in tatters.

What I appear to be
Is not necessarily
What I am.

I manifest prosperity
In thought
Not material.

50. I, ALONE, IS ENOUGH

To be alone
Is not
To be lonely
For in silence
We commune
With our purest thoughts.

When all else
Does not matter
The self
Recedes to itself

That is when
The inner voice
Knocks on the doorstep
Of your soul
It has all the answers
To your worrisome questions

Don't fear
To be alone
The only thing to fear
Is the feeling of loneliness
That arises
Because you have chosen
Not to believe
In the power of the inner voice
For it protects you
Even when you are alone

Listen to the voice
That will emancipate you
From overdependence
On company

Listen to the voice
Of true freedom.

∞

51. WHEN THE UNEXPECTED HAPPENS

When the unexpected happens
Breath properly

When the unexpected happens
Surprise surfaces
Then disappears
After the incubation
Of reality

When the unexpected happens
Change
Rears its head
And calls for attention

When the unexpected happens
Vibration and energy
Shifts
To a new vantage point
Calling for a rethink
Of the status quo

When the unexpected happens
The universe calls
For a change

In perspective
Just unexpectedly
As the unexpected happening.

∞

52. I WILL NOT MOURN

I will not mourn
The death of a loved one
As if I have lost a treasure
For the treasure in the soul
Remains intact
It only transits
To another realm

I will not mourn
The death of a loved one
As if all is lost
For there is no endedness
All that fades away
Returns to shine more brighter
Obscured from the human eye
But exuberant
In a higher realm of existence
More grander
Than the allure
Of the pleasures of this world

I will not mourn
The death of a loved one
But celebrate

A life
Well lived on earth
But now elevated
To a glorious pedestal
Of eternity.
(In honour of Kenyan cabinet ministers who died in a helicopter crash)

∞

53. IT IS NOT THE PRAISE

It is not the praise
That lifts my spirits
But the joy
Of exercising my abilities
To fulfill
My mission
Of realizing
Who I truly am

It is not the praise
That lifts my spirits
But the feeling
Of exhilaration
Of sharing my gifts
With those who need them
It redeems my soul
To put my talents
At the service
Of those who appreciate them most.

It is not the praise
That lifts my spirits
But the conviction
To make a contribution

To the betterment
Of a disenchanted lot
Who see
Only misery and suffering

It is not the praise
That lifts my spirits
But the knowledge
That the desires of this world
Are all achievable
With the alignment of vibration
To the source energy

Yes,
It is not the praise
It is the knowledge.

∞

54. THE BEING, THE MYSTERIOUS

Every human being
Is a great mystery

That is why
You will never see another being
Like you
I know
That I am special

My replica
Is impossible

My uniqueness
Is the image of God
The mysterious.

∞

55. WHAT IS IN A COLOUR?

You painted me black
And yourself white

Have you heard of the hue
Or better still
The rainbow?

Every colour
Is a colour

It seems
That we are all coloured
Black, white, brown

Nobody wants to be colourless
So
What is in a colour?
Is it nothing
And everything
At the same time?

There is nothing
To anything
Wake up.

56. UNTITLED

What is observed
Is affected
By the observer
So
Be careful
About what you choose
To observe.

∞

57. KNOWLEDGE

Vibrational match
Occurs to you
Whether you know it
Or not

The beauty of it
Is that
When you recognize
A vibrational match
In your experience
Magic manifests.

It is good
To know
That knowledge
Is life itself
Treasure it.

∞

58. ILLUSIONS

Illusions
Of grandeur
Are just that
Illusions.

Anything tangible
Is focused imagination
That is the cornerstone
Of deliberate creation.

59. APPRECIATION

Appreciation
Is the truest
And highest
Form of alignment
To the source energy

It reveals
The inner beauty
Of the human soul

Unadulterated
By undesirable thoughts

It is the closest
Human beings have come
To being GOD.

60. THE INVISIBLE WEALTH

Money and power
You acquire them
Here on earth
And leave them here
When you finally exit
The planet
You leave
With your soul
Intact
For it is the perfect repository
Of freedom
From the hunger
For materiality.

61. NOTHING BUT THE SOUL

I have thought of nothing else
Other than loving you

I have thought of nothing else
Other than worshipping you

I have thought of nothing else
Other than listening to you

I have thought of nothing else
Other than trusting you

Oh
My beloved soul
What would I do
Without you?

∞

62. OPEN RACE

There is no competition
Even when the world
Is awash
With all manner of duels
The race
Is not be won
Because there is no end
To an open race

No one
Wins a race
That has no prize

This race
Continues
FOREVER

Keep running
Or just keep walking

You will never be late
Just keep walking
There is no finishing tape
Keep walking

This is not a race
For the faint hearted

The real marathon
Has just began

Do you still want
To continue with a race
That has no competition?

That is the true meaning
Of living.

63. ENDLESS LOVE

You can fall in love
With anyone
Anywhere
Anytime.

Love
Does not know time

Time
Is a creation of mankind
For convenience

Love
Is boundless.

64. HONESTY

If you truly believe
In somebody
You do so
So deeply
That there is no room
For disbelief
Follow your heart.

∞

65. NOBODY KNOWS

Nobody
Knows the future

Nobody
Predicts the future

The future
Unfurls itself
As dictated
By the source energy

Vibration
Is the future
Because
You vibrate
Every time

So
NOW
Is the future.

∞

66. THAT IS THE WAY IT GOES

In walking
You learn

In sleeping
You dream

In standing
You still

In meditation
You release

In visualization
You activate

In affirmation
You ignite, activate and concretize

In writing
You validate

In singing
You record and epitomize

That is just the way
Life goes.

67. TO WIN A WAR

What is
To win a war?

Is it
Decimating a whole army
And proclaiming supremacy
Over uncountable corpses?

Is it
Toppling a regime
That has been butchering and mistreating
Its citizens
And replacing it
With a tolerant one?

Is it
Finding a cure
For the most debilitating malady
On earth?

Is it
Killing all homosexuals
And declaring a gay-free republic?

Is it
Putting a moratorium
On all poaching activities
Around the globe?

Is it
Winning a contract
Due to powerful connections
Regardless of the due procedure?

Is it
Winning a political context
In a free and fair election
Where the ballot
Is the decider
Of victory?

Is it
Quitting alcoholism
And embracing teatotalling?

Is it
Acquiring
An academic degree?

Is it
Amassing wealth?

Is it
Defeating an opponent
In a match?

Is it
Caring for orphaned children
By offering them
Food and a warm bed?

You tell me
What is
To win a war?

∞

68. TRUTH

Truth
Is encased
In mystery.
Unravelling it
Is the business
Of life.

69. FALLING FROM THE SKY

All manner of things
Are falling from the sky
If only I could allow
And receive them

All manner of things
Are falling from the sky
May I not
Cloud my thinking
With imaginary scarcity

All manner of things
Are falling from the sky

Falling
To be received and appreciated
All manner of things
Are falling from the sky
What have I caught?

All manner of things
Are falling from the sky
Falling into open arms

All manner of things
Are yours
Look up
And embrace
And receive them
All manner of things
Are falling from the sky.

∞

70. A GENEROUS HEART

A generous heart
Is a large vessel
That pumps blessings
Into its arteries
And fills it
With abundant life

A generous heart
Expands the love of humanity.
It envelopes
The entire universe.

A generous heart
Is God
The being.

∞

71. SUPREMACY OF INSPIRATION

There is nothing
More enthralling
Than an inspiring friend
Who urges one's creativity
To peter out
From a mountain
Of uncertainty

A model
To emulate
Is much more
Than a pile of money
For inspiration
Distills one's potential
Into concrete success
While wealth simply evaporates
In thin air.

∞

72. I AM NOT AFRAID

I am not afraid
That I will run out of money

I am not afraid
That I will run out of processions

I am not afraid
That I will run out of friends

I am not afraid
That I will run out of fame

I am not afraid
That I will run out of power and authority

The only thing
That I am so afraid of
Is running out
IDEAS.

∞

73. IMAGINE AND MANIFEST

It looks inappropriate
To pretend
That you are
What you are not

But
It is not bad at all
To pretend
That wellbeing
Flows in you
For the universe
Does not respond
To whatever experience
You are living now
But the vibration you offer
Even when you just imagine it.

Wouldn't it be nice
To practice and determine
Your feeling place
And pivot it
Towards abundance?

∞

74. EVERY DEATH IS A SUICIDE

You can never die
Before giving a vibrational consent
By stopping
To make decisions
About the physical world

That withdrawal
Willingly
Of consent
Is a transition
That guarantees
The next vantage point

That withdrawal
Reverts the soul
To its original source
The non physical energy

So
It is not so bad
After all
I am not afraid
Of commiting this suicide
Do not mourn me

Because
I will be going back
To where I came from.

75. GOD IS ONE

How do you know
What you want
Without the knowledge
Of what you do not want?

You must know
The darker side
Before you can see the light
Even Paul
Was Saul
Before Damascus

You can only extinguish the light
To experience darkness

Divine dichotomy
Is the rule
Without exception
Every manifestation

Arises
Out of attention
And intention.

76. LISTENING IS ALLOWING

It is not the loud
Who get the most
In a discussion.

Instead,
It is the quite,receptive and attentive
Lot
Who imbibe
The wisdom
That is encased
In speeches.

To listen
Is to allow
The alignment
To the source energy.
Listen and live.

77. LOVE AND LIGHT

To despise a hero
Is like ignoring a gem
Right at your doorstep.

There is no benefit
To ill feeling
Because
When you appreciate,
The universe expands
And we all gain

When will you learn
That the source energy
Excludes no one

You cannot bring darkness
To a sparkling spectacle
That is embedded
In LIGHT.

∞

78. WE ARE ONE

You can connect
With anything
From any part of this globe

Distance
Is an illusion
That mankind has grafted
In their psyche

Words travel
And with them
The spirit endures

You are my brother
And sister
More than you have ever believed

How come
That you feel comfortable
Where you were not born?

The only reason
Is that you have moved so expansively
To restrict yourself

To where you were originally born
We are ONE.

79. WRITING IS MY RIGHT

Do I imagine
And write
Or do I write
What I observe
In real time?

I write
What I feel
Is valuable and pleasurable
To me

What I feel
After the experience of writing
Is joy and happiness

What I write
Is my absolute choice
Even when you don't approve

What I write
Is my essence
Even when you think otherwise
What I write
Communicates the workings of my inner being
Even when you see it as a triviality

What I write
Is a demonstration of my eternal connection
to the source energy
Even when you chide at it as a joke.

What I write
Is my truest attempt to demonstrate my
commitment to realizing
Who I truly am
Even when you dismiss it as an idle exercise

What I write
Is my right.

∞

80. CHOICE OF WAR

You don't have
To feel bad all the time
You can pivot.

The only reason
Humanity exists
Is bliss
Even when they deny it

What could be more blissful
Than focusing one's thoughts
On good feeling moments
Then manifest them
In PEACE
For all of us?
It can be done

Yes
The world is at war
By CHOICE.

∞

81. EVERYDAY IS A NEW DAY

Everyday
Is a new day
Never go to bed
Expecting things
To unravel in the same way
On the following day

Everyday
Offers its vibration
In relation
To how you offer yours

Everyday
You can choose
To offer vibration
That aligns
To the source energy

Everyday
Is a new day
A fresh place.

∞

82. WAKE UP

The energy vibrates
Whether you are aware of it
Or not

You
Are in a position
To direct your thoughts

Do you want your thoughts
To wander aimlessly
And lead you to the pit?

Pay attention
To how you feel
And the thoughts
That make you feel that way.

∞

83. MATTERS OF THE HEART

Matters of the heart
Are not for sale
Anywhere in the world.
What is on sale
Are matters of the flesh.

Matters of the heart
Are not negotiable
In a free market
Where the willing buyer
Willing seller mantra
Reigns supreme

Matters of the heart
Resonate with intuition
That inner feeling
That knows no tangible gold.

Matters of the heart
Are not for sale.

∞

84. IT ONLY HAPPENS ONCE

It is that one brushstroke
That creates a masterpiece.

It is that one poem
That rattles a people
Into reality.

It is that one song
That pricks the conscience of all
To change their ways.

It is that one speech
That pierces the heart of militants
To drop their guns.

It is that one thought
That will change the universe
FOREVER.

It happens
Just
ONCE.

∞

85. GOD IS SOUL

Every soul
Is a great mystery.

Every soul
Is good.

Every soul
Is an extension of the source energy.

Every soul
Is sacred and sacrosanct.

Every soul
Is a manifestation of wellbeing.

Every soul
Is GOD.

∞

86. THOUGHT IS LIFE

Everything
That is anything
Is that thing
Because
It has been thought
Into being
By somebody.

So
Create your own reality
By thinking it
Into being.

Truth is relative
And
Thought is life.

∞

87. GIVE THANKS

When everybody elese
Is complaining
Give thanks.

When everybody else
Is grieving
Give thanks.

When everybody else
Is criticizing
Give thanks.

When everybody else
Is condemning
Give thanks.

When everbody else
Is worrying
Give thanks.

Give thanks
All the time
No matter the circumstance.

88. FEEL THE EXPECTATION

Wait
For what you desire
In anticipation.

Do not worry
About how what you desire
Will happen.

Just pay attention
To how you feel
About what you desire.

When you think about
What you desire,
Doubting and worrying
Whether it will happen,
You offer resistance
To the manifestation
Of your desire.

∞

89. DO IT WITH PRIDE

Do it with pride
No matter what it is
White collar or otherwise
For it is not the trade
But the contribution.

Do it with pride
No matter the paycheck
For your satisfaction
Is not dependently
Only on gold and silver
There is much more to it.

Do it with pride
Because it has never been about
What you are doing
But how you feel
When you are doing
What you always do.

Do it with pride
And feel good.

∞

90. LEADERSHIP

Leadership
Is not about
Wielding power
And authority.

It
Is not about being praised,garlanded
And decorated
With all sorts of adornments.

It
Is not about
Kowtoing to kith
And kinsmen.

It
Is not about
Issuing edicts and decrees.

It
Is not about
Silencing opponents
And other dissenting voices.

It
Is not about
Amassing a mound of fortune.

It
Is not about
Ascending to the throne
And inheriting a birthright.

Leadership
Is about initiative
And service.

∞

91. DONT WORRY

Do not worry
About the time
That you have wasted
For there is no
Endedness.

Do not worry
About what
You are yet to achieve
For rockets of desire
Will continue to spew forth
Out of your preferences
Unceasingly.

Do not worry
About being lesser than others
For you can be do or have
Anything you want
So long as you offer vibration
That aligns
To the source energy.

Do not worry
Because you are here

To joyously create
And enjoy the experience.

Focusing on other people
Robs you the power
To focus on
The endless possibilities
Encased
In your very own being.

Do not worry
About anything
For there is nothing
To anything.
Just enjoy the ride
As if nobody existed
In your world.

∞

92. SEA OF CALM

Have you watched the sea
Calm?
Have you also watched the sea
Turbulent,like a tsunami?

Everything
Is two faced

Have wished
To be
In a sea of calm?
Which sea do you want
To see?

∞

93. A WARM RAIN

Would you brave
A warm rain
Now that a cold one
Scares you senseless?

Every drop
Of cold water
Smashes life
Into your consciousness
It awakes you.

So
Would you still brave
A warm rain?

I have never seen
A thoroughly cold rained, sleepy
Being
Have you?

∞

94. CURIOSITY

Do you know
How difficult it is
To kill a creature
With nine lives?

But
Curiosity
Still killed
The cat

So
Look less and imagine more
That way,
You will never attract
What you don't want to experience
By looking at it.

∞

95. WELLNESS

Your wellbeing
Entirely depends
On your vibration
And not
The manifestation
Of the vibration.

Start thinking
About how to raise and maintain
The level of your vibration
And not
How you will feel
When the manifestation
Occurs.

Continue
Refining the picture
Instead of
Focussing on the marvel
Of the picture
Because life is
ENERGY.

∞

96. LIFE

Life
Is one long day
It
Is one long season

It
Is not segmented
Into months and years

It
Is a journey
That does not end
With the end
Of physical life

It
Is a continuum
Exhibited
In the form of
Transformations
That easily confuse the eye
As an end

Life
Is eternal.

97. WHY ARE YOU AFRAID?

Why are you afraid
Of giving the world
What it is looking for?

Why are you worried
About people knowing
What you know?

Are you not aware
That every human being
Is unique and at the same time
Colourfully independent?

Why have you been thinking
That everybody
Has to witness
The day you make a date
With the source energy?

It has never been
A crowd thing

Why do you think
That your past

Must be the mirror
Infront of you?

Why not think
Of everyday as a fresh place
Where creation
Manifests?

Why do you create
What you don't want
Why?

∞

98. TEAMWORK LEADS

You break a heart
Once
So, would you want
To go that path?

Send positive energy
To your aggressors
And assist them
To vibrate positively
For that is how
They can access
Wellbeing.

There is no other way
To lead
Than to offer good energy
That refines
The vision of a team.

You can never lead
By focusing on
Self
At a time
When you are supposed

To focus
On the vibration of all members
Of a team.

When you realize
That what you think
And do
Affects many other souls
You might want to pause
And ask yourself
What energy
Am I offering right now?

Don't create misery
When you can
Bliss
Willingly.

∞

99. I AM WHOLE

I am whole
There is no void
To fill.

I am on top
There is no mountain
To climb.

I am love
There is no soul
To conquer.

I am freedom
There are no chains
To unshackle.

I am power
There is no force
To subdue.

I am knowledge
There is nothing to learn
Only to remember.

I am the perfect creation
Do I know it?

100. THE OMEN

If you can see a life
Out there in the desert
Then you can find
Your treasure.

Because life attracts life
You ended up
Here
In the desert.

If you know
The language of life
Then you can live
Anywhere.

Pursue your omen
And discover
Your personal legend
Your eternal goal
On this planet earth.

101. I KNOW

I know
That I have to let you go
Because men go
In order to return.

But I also know
That you will always be
My eternal treasure.

So
Go and find whatever it is
You are looking for.

Your treasure
Is mine too
FOREVER.

∞

102. WAIT FOR ME

I love you so much
To see you believe
That this all I am.

Let me go
And I will return
Better than anything
You have ever imagined
Wait for me.

103. MAKE MORE MONEY

If you want to make more money
You must be able
To control your emotions.

How do you control
The flow of money
In your life
When you cannot
Control
The vibration of energy
That leads to abundance?

How do you feel
When you have tonnes
Of money?
And
How do you feel
When you lose
All of it?

You can only increase
The flow of money
In your life
By aligning yourself
To the source energy.

If you want to be rich
Start paying attention to
Your point of assemblage
Because it determines
Whether you will strike riches
Or die trying.

∞

104. SALVATION

Have you ever thought
About the real meaning
Of salvation?

What is the true essence
Of salvation?
Should it be internal?
Or otherwise
Does it have
Something to do with celebration
Of self?

True love
Of self
And others
Is the real bedrock
Of salvation.

Must somebody nudge you
To experience salvation?
Or
Is it something
That you activate
In you

By relaxing and allowing
The manifestation
Of how you really feel
About everybody and everything
Around you?

105. ARE YOU REALLY HAPPY?

Are you really happy?
What is your happiness
Premised on?
Is it based on recognition
Or
A sense of self worth?

Are you really happy?
When you have to wait
For somebody else
To recognize you
In order to create
A sense of joy
In your being?

Are you really happy?
When you flaunt ego
As the cornerstone
Of your perceived wellbeing?

Are you really happy?
When you fill the void
You have created in you
With material?

Happiness
Is like a butterfly
It will always
Elude itself from you
If you concentrate on something
The butterfly will come
And perch itself
On your shoulders

Never premise
Your happiness
On any condition
Love is unconditional.

106. THERE IS NO RETIREMENT

There is no retirement
In life.

When you decide
To retire,
You give away
Your ability
To create.

When you retire
You start dying
Even when
You are still breathing.

There is no retirement
In life.
There is only
Being and living
Eternally.

∞

ABOUT THE AUTHOR

JACOB O OKETCH

Jacob Oketch is a practicing print journalist in Nairobi, Kenya. He has participated in several writers' workshops and seminars. Currently, he is the treasurer of PEN-Kenya. He is also a performing artist; performs poetry and he is also a storyteller. This is his first collection of poetry.